I0468942

**Adwoa Asiedu Foreword by Bishop Michael Hutton-Wood**

**Senior Pastor of House OF Judah Praise Ministries, President of Michael Hutton-Wood Ministries and Director of Leader's Factory International**

**Lyrics From Within Volume 2**

**A Collection of 25 Lyrics Written by Adwoa Asiedu**

# Foreword

The deeper one's relationship with God, the sweeter and deeper the words, the expression, the communion and the richer and more genuine the love that can be felt in the words spoken in poems and songs written as genuine expressions of this love.

From the expressions of love, gratitude and the testimonies, you cannot help but feel, sense and be inspired and blessed by the depth of intimacy that flows through these poems. The scripture is so true that he who is forgiven much loves much and a man or woman's gift indeed makes room for them.

I believe Adwoa's gift will make room for her, bless thousands and bring her before great men just like the gifts of Joseph, Daniel, David and Deborah brought them into prominence.

Well done Adwoa and more grace!

**Bishop Michael Hutton-Wood**

**Senior Pastor of House of Judah Praise Ministries, President of Michael Hutton-Wood Ministries and Director of Leader's Factory International**

# About The Author

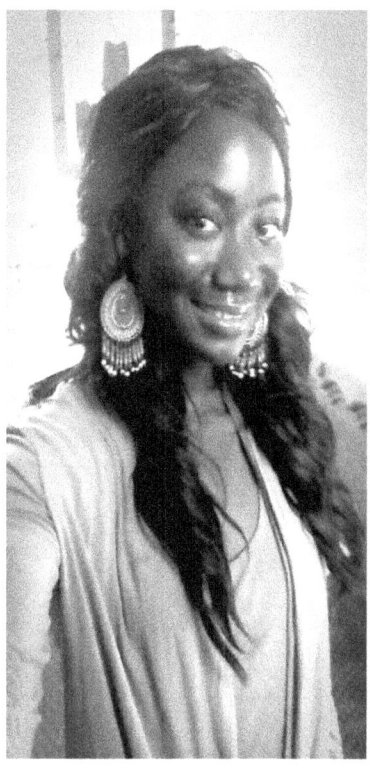

The Author Adwoa Asiedu is an English Language, Communications and Sociology graduate from Canterbury Christ Church University, England.

Multi-Talented Adwoa Asiedu is a poet, lyricist, screenwriter, writer and singer. Adwoa Asiedu is also the Founder and Executive Director of 'From Within Project'. Follow the Inspiring movement by liking the Facebook page:
https://www.facebook.com/FromWithinAdwoaAsiedu/

Adwoa Asiedu has completed a screenwriting course led by Award Winning Screenwriter and Film Director Maeve Murphy. Other Credentials include publishing her Debut Book of Lyrics: Lyrics From Within Volume 1- A Collection of 26 lyrics written by Adwoa Asiedu in May 2015 Foreword written by Peter Russell- Chaplain of St Lawrence College, Ramsgate, Kent. Kindle and Paperback versions are available to purchase on amazon.com.

Adwoa Asiedu also published her Debut Book of Poems in October 2014- From Within Volume 1- A Collection of 54 Poems including 15 Published Poems. Foreword written by Olubanke King Akerele - Former Minister of Foreign Affairs. Kindle and Paperback versions available to purchase on amazon.com

Adwoa Asiedu has worked as a Contributing Editor for 4 Printed Volumes of Ten2Teens Magazine and is presently blogging for Me Firi Ghana - A Leading Brand Connecting people to Ghana.

# Acknowledgements

My sincere gratitude to **Bishop Michael Hutton-Wood** for writing a lovely and precise foreword. I'm thankful that God has blessed you with great wisdom and a contagious sense of humour. May God continue to use you to bless so many people particularly my generation.

Thank you to **Pastor Eddie Rowlands** for all your prayers and support whilst I was fellowshipping at **New Life Family Church in Margate, Kent**.

Thank you to **House of Judah Prayer Team** for all your support and prayers.

Thank you to the **Prayer Team** at **Ramsgate Christian Fellowship** for all their support and prayers especially **Pastor Anthony Pearse**, **Pam**, **Sandra** and **Joyce**.

Thank you to my Father **Dr John James Kojo Asiedu** for all your love and support.

Thank you to my Mother **Dorothy Asiedu** for all your love and support.

Thank you to my brothers **Kwabena and Kwaku Asiedu** for all your love and support.

Thank you to my Grandad **Ernest Boateng** for all your love and support.

Thank you to **Apostle Opoku and Muriel Opoku** for your support and prayers.

Thank you to **KICC Prayer Team** for all your support and prayers.

Thank you to **Nazma Mahomed and Fareed Mahomed** for your continuous love and support towards me.

Thank you to **Rayeesa Leila Mahomed my sister**. You have such a beautiful heart. You bring out the best in me. Thank you for always being there for me.

Thank you to **Nicole Margarita Henworth my diva.** Thank you for being a great supportive friend. You are so special and I'm blessed to have you in my life.

Thank you to these guys who are like brothers to me. I'm thankful for their continuous support: **Joshua Thompson**, **Fifi Botchway**, **Oblie Botchway**, **Joshua Botchway**, **Kitor Carew and Kareem Abu Shams.**

Thank you to **Me Firi Ghana Team: Arnold-Sarfo Kantaka, Ben Antwi, Yaa Narko** and the rest of the team for all the love and support.

A special thank you to these wonderful people who have shown support and love:

**Elizabeth Ejaife, Mary Ejaife, Joanna Howard-Field, Kenneth I Koyoma, Holly Archer, Ruth Rayner, Stephen Rayner, Giona Gaituah, Michael Amaning, Christina Swaby and Christine van der Linden.**

# Introduction

Hello World!

Welcome to the next chapter of my journey – **Lyrics From Within Volume 2**!

Lyrics From Within Volume 2 reveals a more passionate side to my writing and it highlights Fierce Anthems, Love Songs and Songs of Worship.

These volumes of lyrics show my vulnerability as a writer. The scary thing about this is that Writing exposes you. I always think if you really want to know someone, then read what they write because it gives you clues about who they are and what they represent.

In this volume of lyrics, I am able to reveal my weaker sides. I am not afraid of being vulnerable with my writing because it frees me.

I trust in the word that says in 2 Corinthians 12: 9 "My grace is sufficient for you, for my power is made perfect in weakness." Therefore I will boast all the more gladly about my weaknesses, so that Christ's power may rest on me.

The message for you my readers is to not be afraid to be vulnerable. There is beauty in vulnerability. In the world that we live in today, people put on a mask afraid of being seen as 'weak' but I dare you to remove the mask and let people see you!

If you are on Facebook, Follow the inspiring **From Within Project by Adwoa Asiedu** and be a part of this new exciting movement!

**Spread the word: From Within**

Love you all,

Adwoa Asiedu

### 1. Look At Me

Look at me

What do you see?

Look at me again

Do you see what I see


The veil is stripping away

No longer hiding from me

This new light shining is me

Can you believe it?


Yes this is me

Coming out darkness

Throw me to the light

I'm ready to dream

I'm ready to live


Look at me

What do you see?

Look at me again

Do you see what I see

Anoint me all over with fresh oil


Daughter Arise and Shine

For your light has come

Yes your light has come

## 2. Will You Lift The Veil?

Spirit hover over the earth

You spoke and said

Let there be light

And there was light


Living in a world of confusion

People afraid of the truth

Afraid of being exposed


Father, you are our Father

We are simply dust

Lift the veil

So we can see


Lift the veil from our eyes

Let us see one another with your eyes

Let us see each other as brothers and sisters

Not as enemies or strangers


Will you lift the veil?

Will you lift the veil?

Will you lift the veil?

Will you lift the veil?

### 3.  Jump Over The River

Is this my girl crying?

The sound of your tears makes my heart sad

The storm is over now

This is your season


If you feel things are still the same

You say that nothing is improving

You know what you have to do  right?

What ? Jump !

You need to jump!


So jump over the river , Don't stop

Jump over the river

Jump over the river


You have been walking for so long

Now I dare you to jump

If you jump this year

You will not be in the same spot

As last year

So I dare you to jump


So jump over the river, don't stop

Jump over the river

Jump over the river

### 4. Who Can Compare To You?

Choosing to ignore them

Choosing to live my life

A life that pleases you


You are the only one I need

The lover of my soul

Who can compare to you?

Who can compare to you ?


At times I feel the rest of the world are just spying

Not really contributing or showing love

Just spying, looking to see my next move


Looking to you only

Trusting you to guide me

Trusting you to protect me


I am the apple of your eye

Forever will I sing:

Who can compare to you

Who can compare to you

## 5. Rise Up

Taking my place

Not going to be who I was

Can't be where I was


I hear you say

Rise up

I hear you say

Rise up

It's your turn

It's your turn


Been waiting for a moment like this

You kept me in the dark

Had to go through the ugly seasons

To get to where I am today

You had to prune me from everything

That is not pleasing to you


Today I ask let there be light

Light in my dreams

Light in my aspirations


I hear him say

Rise up, rise up

### 6. Deliver Me

From wicked men

From cheaters

From exploiters


We live in a dark world

Spirit come

Change the atmosphere


I won't leave without you


It's you and I

You and I against the world

(Deliver me from this world)


Lead me

Guide me

Hold my hand as we do this together


I won't leave without you


Cause it's you and I

You and I against the world

(Deliver me from this world )

## 7.  He Is Good

I remember when I first started

I didn't know what I was doing

I didn't know what you were doing

I was lost


Scared of the unknown

but You came through

Yes You came through


Learning to trust you

So I give you praise

My heart will testify

Oh how He's good


You're full of surprises

 Oh He is good

He is good, He is good, He is good

Oh He is good

He is good, He is good, He is good.

## 8. Father Of Creation

In my generation, let hope arise

In my generation, let there be light

Break forth like a mighty wind

We need you more than ever

We are your people, we are yours

Hearts fully surrendered to you

We lift you up, up!

Father of creation

We lift you up, up!

Our Father hallowed be your name

The name above all names

Jesus , the mystery of creation

Your kingdom come

Your will be done

We lift you up,up!

Father of creation

We lift you up,up!

### 9. Dear Child Of Destiny

Baby don't you cry

I know your story

It happened to make you stronger


See my child,

You are representing me

Before I release you

I need you to be strong


This is for the world to see

The is for the world to know

I am the Alpha and Omega

Your beginning and your end


Dear Child of Destiny, I have a plan for you

Dear Child of Destiny, have faith and believe


Dear Child of Destiny, I love you

## 10. Set It Ablaze

Waking up today with a new vision

Full of expectations

Today is going to be a great day


Oooooh I feel on top of the world

Oooooh you can't quench this fire


Set it ablaze ( Consume me )

Set it ablaze (Consume me )

Set it ablaze (Consume me )


You are my joy

You are my life

Just want my life to be filled with  your glory


Hallelujah to the King of Kings

Hallelujah to the Lord of Lords

Hallelujah (4)

## 11. You Know You're Beautiful

You know you're beautiful (baby)

You know you're beautiful (baby)


Have I met you before?

Your face seems familiar

Your smile tells me

Maybe we've met

In your dreams?

Or in mine?


Don't have time to play

Been there before (Don't remind me )

Worst mistake of my life

But learnt the best lesson


I refuse to be treated as a $2^{nd}$ option

It's me or nothing baby


You know you're beautiful (baby)

You know You're beautiful  (baby)

## 12. This Is My Hometown

Let there be laugher (in this hometown)

Let there be love (in this hometown)

Unite us as one

So we can stand as one!


We are a people

We are one race

Open the blind eyes

So they can see that we are one

Yes we are one ooooh

We are one yeah


This is my hometown

I shine, I shine

This is my hometown

I shine, I shine


Here for a reason

You can't stop me

I shine to give you glory

This is my hometown


Wherever my feet land, I reign, I reign

### 13.  Take A Risk

What are you afraid of?

You never know until you try

What are you worrying for?

Don't you know it's a crime


To worry, to panic for what?

Your future is in His hands


Baby fly away

So take a risk

And take your place

You  will soar like an eagle

So Rise

Higher higher

Yes I see me


Watch me run away

Watch me run away

Watch me run away


From my fears

Watch me run away

From my past

Watch me run away

## 14. I Hear

That Day is going to be our day

Our Day where no one will get in the way

Where all eyes would be on us

There our story would unfold


You know the skies will rejoice with us

Cause it's going to be our day


I hear, I hear

The heavens singing over us

Singing over us

Singing over us

I hear, I hear


This will be a day we won't forget

A day to rewrite our story

Our day to cry together

Our day to laugh together


You know the skies will rejoice with us

Cause it's going to be our day

I hear, I hear

The heavens singing over us

Singing over us

Singing over us

## 15.  Expiry Date

Never thought you and I would part like this
Times and seasons matter to us all

Would you still be here if I had not said anything?

The flame I once had for you is no longer there
Maybe today is the expiry date of our journey
Maybe today is the expiry date of our journey
So don't you cry, please don't you cry

Why act like nothing is wrong
This thing you call love isn't real

The flame I once had for you is no longer there
Maybe today is the expiry date of our journey
Maybe today is the expiry date of our journey
So don't you cry, baby don't you cry


It's who I am, It's who I am
Can't pretend, no I can't pretend
That I'm happy ooooooh

Take me as I am
I won't lie to you
I won't lie to myself
I am not happy
I need to leave

Let me go or else I will end up despising you

Time is running out..
Maybe today is the day
Of our expiry date

## 16. Your Presence

Longing for you and I to be one again

Like how we used to be


Do you remember how we were in love

How I was in awe of you


It was your presence

It was your presence

It was your presence

It was your presence


How I need your presence

More than yesterday

Baby I need you

I need you like water


It was your presence

It was your presence

It was your presence

It was your presence


That drew me in

Now it's your presence which will make me remain in you

Come now …

How I long to see your face

## 17. Run

You're telling me to run

I'm asking where?

And I'm hearing you say: Run


So I will run,

I will run

I will run, run, run

I will run, run, run


In the last lap of this race

I started slow but I'm catching up

So I dare to run to overtake those who have gone ahead


I will be the head and never the tail

I will run this race


So I will run

I will run

I will run, run, run

I will run, run, run

## 18. Let Me See You Smile

In the years to come

Will you look back and smile at how far we've come

Tears were sown

Hearts were cold

What we once said

We can never take back


Blessed are you who now weep

For you will laugh


Let me see you smile, Let me see you smile, Let me see you smile


Yeah you may have a dark past

Did you know your days are getting brighter

You were born to smile even in the darkest seasons

Refuse to be a victim and act like a victor


Blessed are you who now weep

For you will  laugh


Let  me see you smile, Let me see you smile, Let me see you smile

No more pain, no more pain, fight for your happiness

## 19. Yes I Was There, I Will Always Be There

Thinking about the blissful times we shared

It was only yesterday

When we were together, growing together

Young and free

Unashamed and unaware of what tomorrow will be


Yes I was there

I will always be there

Even if you're far away

My heart will always be there


It's great to see how far you've come

Who you have become

Everytime I see you

I still remember who you were

Before the world got to know you


Yes I was there

I will always be there

Even if you're far away

My heart will always be there


It was never a goodbye

Cause I was there, I will always be there

I'll see you again

## 20. This Is You!

I need a drink

Thirsty from you

I can't be free without my cup being full


Where is this water?

I need my healing

I am tired of drinking from other wells

There must be another well greater than the rest


Can you see this fountain flowing?

It's unstoppable and moving so rapidly!

Watch this beautiful fountain

Fearless, This is  you!


Beautiful Fountain

Let it overflow

More than yesterday

Let the waters fall deep within my soul


Can you see this fountain flowing?

It's unstoppable and moving so rapidly!

Watch this beautiful fountain

Fearless, This is  you!

## 21. You See Me

I am free to possess what belongs to me

Cause I am Abraham's seed

Yes I am Abraham's seed

My heart is set apart

And you see me


Not what the world sees

But you see me

You see me

You see me

You created me


Not what the world wants to label me

Cause you formed me

Rejecting every lie from society

Every lie of the enemy

But trusting in Your word


Not what the world sees

But You see me

You see me

You see me

You created me

A Diamond in the rough, I'm your hidden gem

You see me!

## 22. He Calls Me

The other night my heart was heavy
Thinking about how broken my heart was
Then I stumbled upon this word
This one word blew me away
I need to ask you
How can someone like you be in love
With someone like me?

I'm blown away by his sweet love
My Romeo is a real romantic

He calls me
He calls me
He calls me
Hephzibah

Oh how can you delight in me?
How can you?
It doesn't make sense
For you to love me like the way you do
You know that I can never love you back the way you love me
It breaks my heart when I think about it.
But that's why I love you
Because you first loved me

When no one did, when no one cared, When no one paid attention

You deserve my heart, I know you won't break my heart

He calls me
He calls me
He calls me
Hephzibah

## 23. Sing To Me A New Song

Sing to me a new song
A song from within
Don't let fear take place
Not in your heart

Where love is, there is no place for fear

I have set you free from fear
Delivered you from fear
Now I call you my beloved

I died so you can be free
I died so you can live the life you always wanted to live
A life of Purpose
A life of Adventure

I rose so that you may know my power

That same power that raised the dead still lives in you

Sing to me a new song
A song From Within
Sing to me a new song
A song From Within
Let me feel your heart beating for me
Sing to me a new song
A Song From Within
A Song From Within

## 24. Beautiful Warrior

Lift her up from this miry pit

Take her on another level

So she can live again

Now she's in the light

She intends to stay in the light


We have risen, we have risen

From the grave

Our past no longer defines us

We are who you say we are


Call me a beautiful warrior

A woman of grace

Call me a beautiful warrior

A woman of substance


You taught me how to fight for my destiny

You taught how to win

I am who I am because of you


Call me a beautiful warrior

A woman of grace

Call me a beautiful warrior

A woman of substance

## 25. Let Heaven Come

(Spoken Word)

I see the heavens opening

With rain pouring down

Then I hear a sound

A joyful sound

A sound of praise

I see a people of all nations

Standing as one

Proclaiming your word

To your people

I see unity

I see love

Let the vision turn to reality


**Song Chorus:**

Let heaven come

Let heaven come

Let heaven come

www.ingramcontent.com/pod-product-compliance
Lightning Source LLC
Chambersburg PA
CBHW080531190526
45169CB00008B/3115